AF481419

Hex codes, or hexadecimal codes, are a way to represent colors in digital devices and web design. Each hex code refers to a very specific color. A hex color is expressed as a six-digit combination of numbers and letters, preceded by a pound sign or hashtag, defined by its mix of red, green, and blue (RGB). The first two letters or numbers refer to red, the next two refer to green, and the last two refer to blue.

The color values are defined as values between 00 and FF. Hex codes are a universal way to describe colors. This book is specifically about jewel tones.

A is for amber

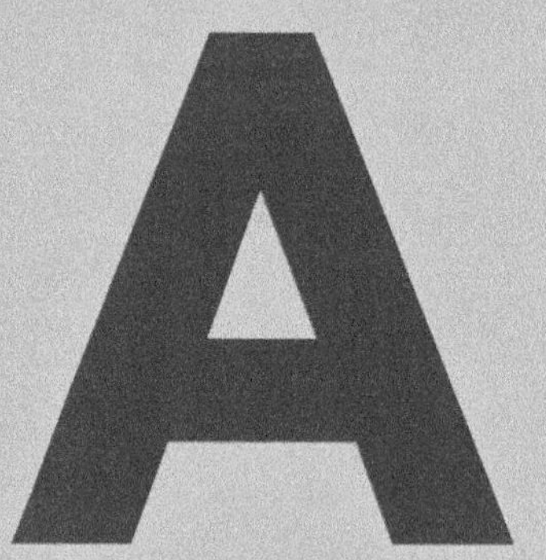

#FFBF00

a is for amethyst

a

#562F7E

B is for blue emerald

B

#0F5A5E

b is for blue opal

b

#0F3B57

C is for cinnabar

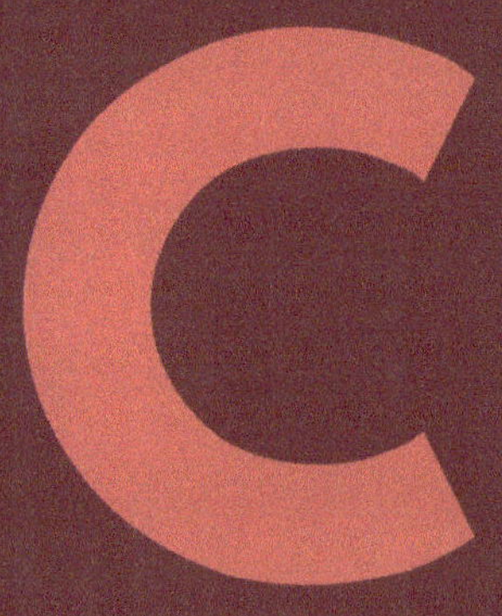

#730113

c is for cruel ruby

C

#DD3344

D is for dark emerald

D

#00834E

d is for diamond blue

d

#CFE4EE

E is for emerald

E

#028F1E

e is for eminence

e

#6C3082

F is for fluorite

F

#B4CCC2

f is for fuchsite

#C3D9CE

G is for garnet

G

#830E0D

g is for gold stone

g

#F6E6B9

H is for hematite

H

#574F50

h is for hessonite

h

#DF6020

I is for imperial topaz

I

#875341

i is for iolite

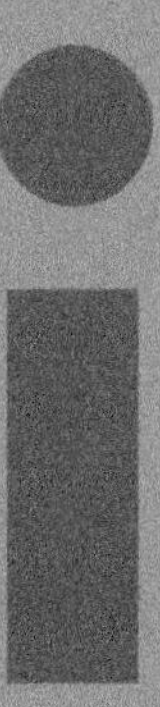

#707BB4

J is for jade

J

#00A86B

j is for jewel

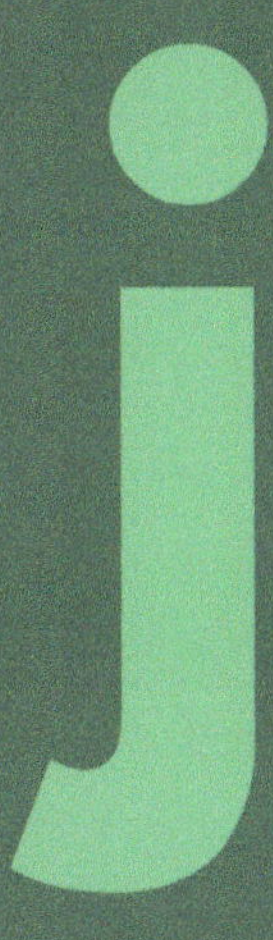

#136843

K is for kunzite

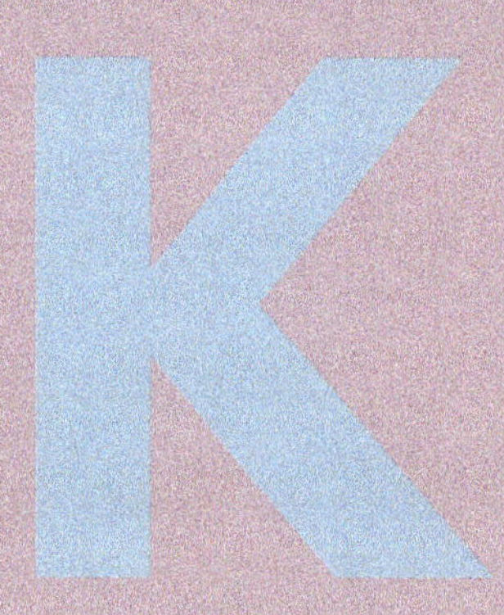

#DDB6C6

k is for kyanite

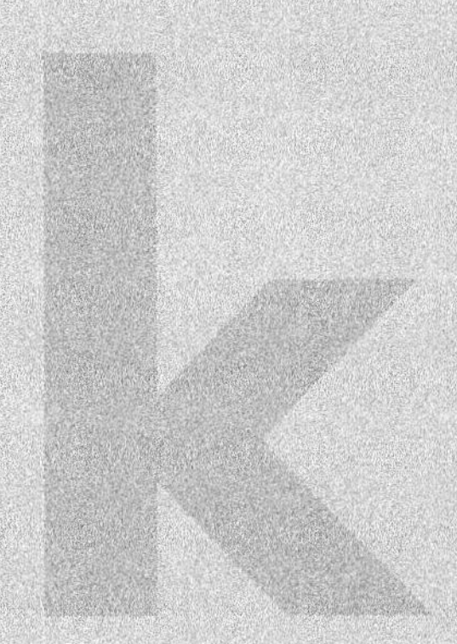

#AAC4DF

L is for lapis lazuli

L

#26619C

l is for larimar

l

#8FD8DE

M is for magnesite

M

#E0DDD7

m is for moldavite

m

#697341

N is for narsarsukite

N

#F7D381

n is for nuummite

n

#1C1D27

O is for onyx

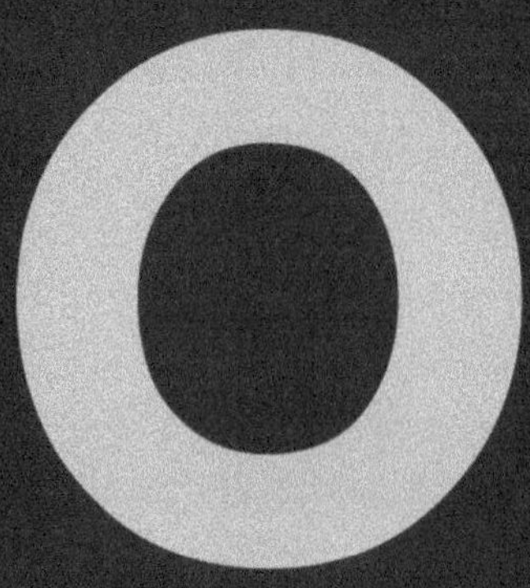

#353839

o is for opal

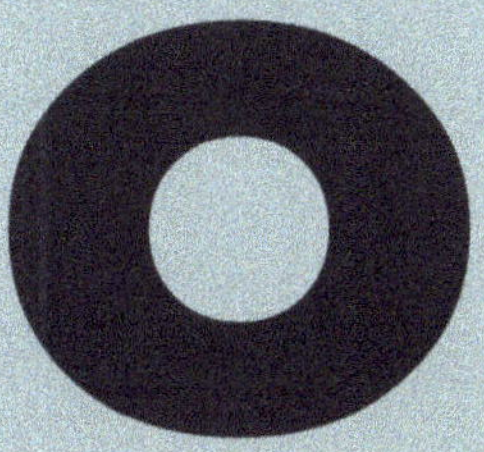

#A8C3BC

P is for pearl

P

#EEFFFF

p is for peridot

p

#B4C424

Q is for quartz

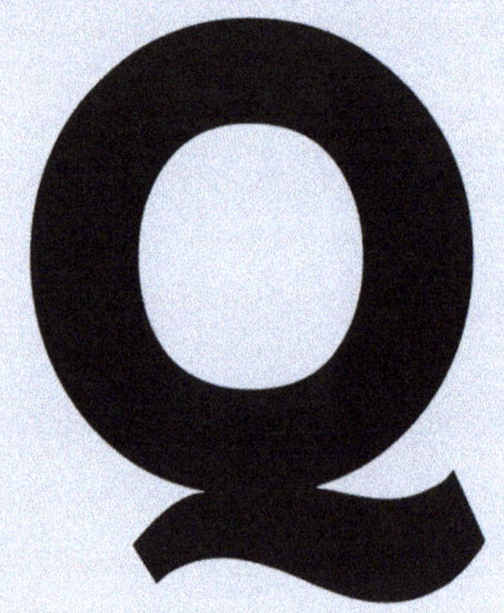

#D9D9F3

q is for quartzite

q

#232E26

R is for rhodonite

R

#C73987

r is for rose quartz

r

#F7CACA

S is for sapphire

S

#0F52BA

s is for sodalite

S

#222D6D

T is for topaz

T

#FFC87C

t is for turquoise

#06C2AC

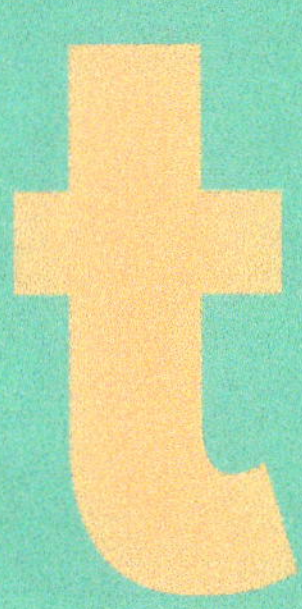

U is for unakite

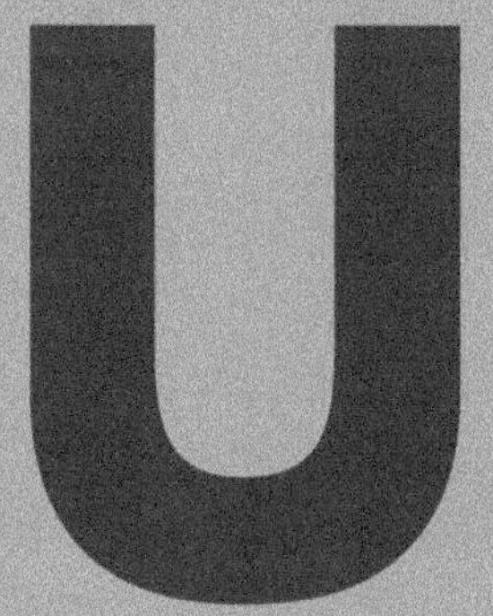

#75A14F

u is for uvarovite

U

#113624

V is for vanadinite

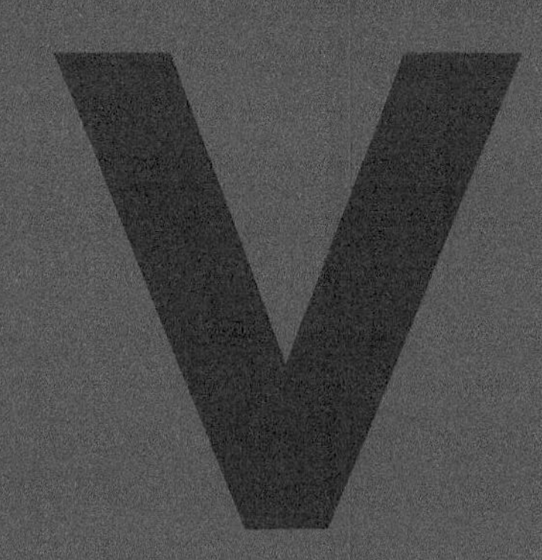

#A60A00

v is for vivianite

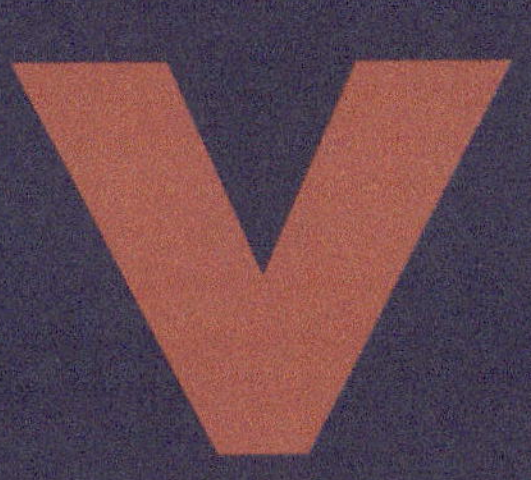

#262B4C

W is for wendwilsonite

W

#CA0866

w is for witherite

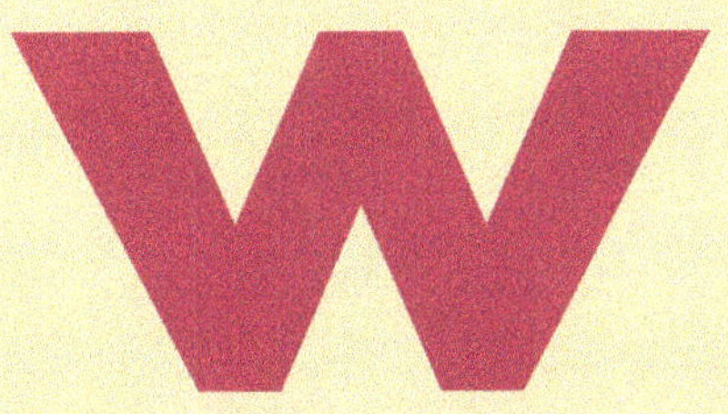

#EEE4AF

X is for xanthite

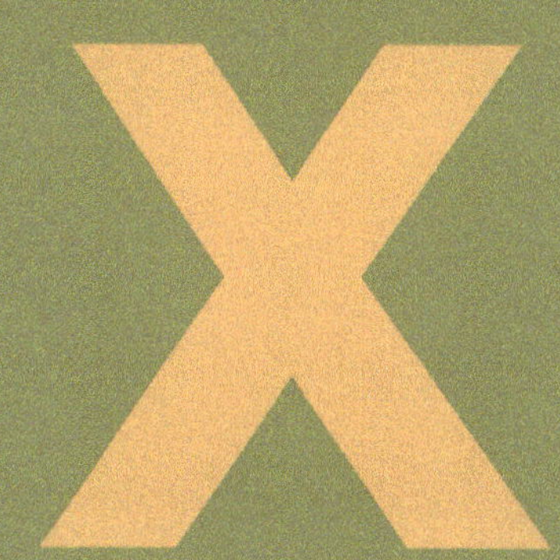

#969644

x is for xenotime

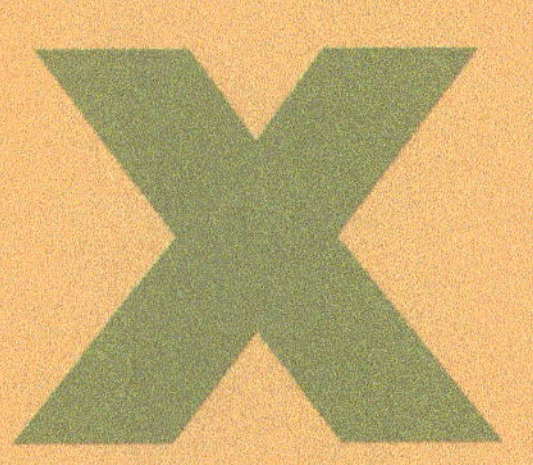

#EFA444

Y is for yttocrasite

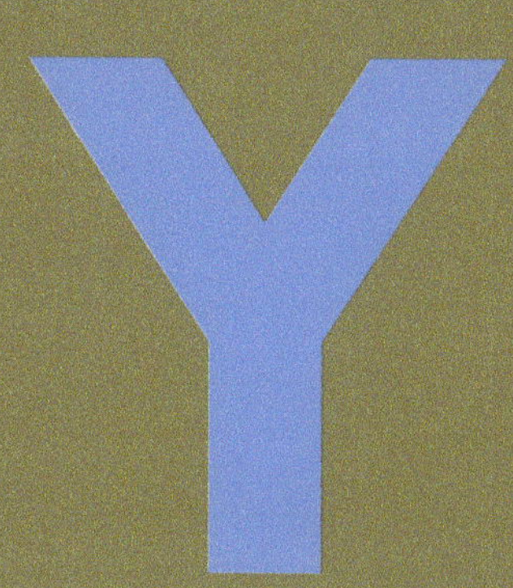

#897D0D

y is for yttrofluorite

y

#576AFE

Z is for zircon

Z

#017082

z is for zoisite

z

#8050E8

9 798868 986352